Alfred's

Music for Little Mozarts

Coloring and Ear Training Activities to ~~Bring~~ Music in Every Young Child

Cover Illustration and Interior art by Christine Finn

Christine H. Barden · Gayle Kowalchyk · E. L. Lancaster

ISBN 0-88284-968-9

Foreword

Recent studies suggest that playing and listening to music at a young age improves learning, memory, reasoning ability and general creativity. Research also supports the theory that young children who are exposed to music develop enhanced cognitive skills. The *Music for Little Mozarts* series was written to provide appropriate piano instruction for four-, five- and six-year-olds while simultaneously developing listening skills. The series was designed to provide a balance between the discipline necessary for playing the instrument and the enjoyment one gets from the process of music-making.

The course centers around the adventures of Beethoven Bear and Mozart Mouse as they learn about music. Three books guide the children through a comprehensive approach to musical learning. In the *Music Lesson Book,* students are introduced to new musical concepts and performance of pieces at the piano as they follow the story of Beethoven Bear and Mozart Mouse. Plush animals of the two characters are integral to making the course fun for young students. The *Music Workbook* contains carefully designed pages to color, that reinforce the musical concepts introduced in the Music Lesson Book. In addition, well-planned listening activities develop ear-training skills. The *Music Discovery Book* contains songs that allow the students to experience music through singing, movement and response to rhythm patterns. Music appreciation is fostered through carefully chosen music

that introduces the students to great music through the ages. Melodies to sing, using either solfege or letter names, help students learn to match pitch and discover tonal elements of music. Correlated compact disc recordings for materials in the Music Lesson and Music Discovery Books are essential to achieve the goals of the course. General MIDI disks also are available for students or teachers who have the necessary equipment. A Starter Kit includes a music bag for carrying lesson materials, a music activity board and the two plush animal characters (Beethoven Bear and Mozart Mouse).

Role of Parents: The teacher serves as a musical guide for young students in fostering their curiosity, natural ability and interest, but parents also play an important role in guiding their child's musical training. The authors recommend that parents attend lessons with their child and participate actively in the learning process. Parents will need to read the directions to their child during daily practice. Regularity of practice is important; short practice sessions of 10–15 minutes are suggested for young students, with activities changing frequently within the practice time. (Teachers can give valuable suggestions regarding practice.) Patience, sincere praise and a show of enthusiasm about new materials will be very beneficial. A musical partnership between parents and child in a nurturing environment provides quality time for fostering important family relationships.

Notes to the Teacher: The course is easy to use both in private and group lessons. Through careful pacing and reinforcement, appealing music with clever lyrics is introduced in the Music Lesson Book. The Music Workbook and Music Discovery Books are correlated page by page with the Music Lesson Book to provide well-balanced lessons. A separate Teacher's Handbook offers suggestions and lesson plans to aid the teacher with planning. All books contain clean and uncluttered pages, clear music engraving and attractive artwork to complement the music and appeal to young children.

About the Music Workbook, Book 1: The Music Workbook reinforces each concept presented in the Music Lesson Book through carefully designed pages for children to color. It also specifically focuses on the training and development of the ear. (Suggested listening examples for ear training pages are given in the Teacher's Handbook.) This book is coordinated page by page with the Music Lesson Book and assignments are ideally made according to the instructions in the upper right corner of each page of the Music Workbook. Many students enjoy completing these pages so much that they will want to work beyond the assigned material. However, it is best to wait until the indicated pages in the Music Lesson Book have been covered before the corresponding material in this book is studied.

The authors and publisher of this course offer our best wishes to children, parents and teachers as you begin this new adventure. It is certain to be richly rewarding!

Table of Contents

Use with Alfred's *Music for Little Mozarts*, Lesson Book 1, page 4.

Making Friends with Beethoven Bear and Mozart Mouse

Beethoven Bear and Mozart Mouse (our music friends) will be our guides throughout *Music for Little Mozarts*.

Color them to match your bean bag animals.

Curve Your Fingers!

Show Beethoven Bear and Mozart Mouse which hand below
has good curved fingers for playing the piano.

● Circle the hand that has good curved fingers with a **red** crayon.

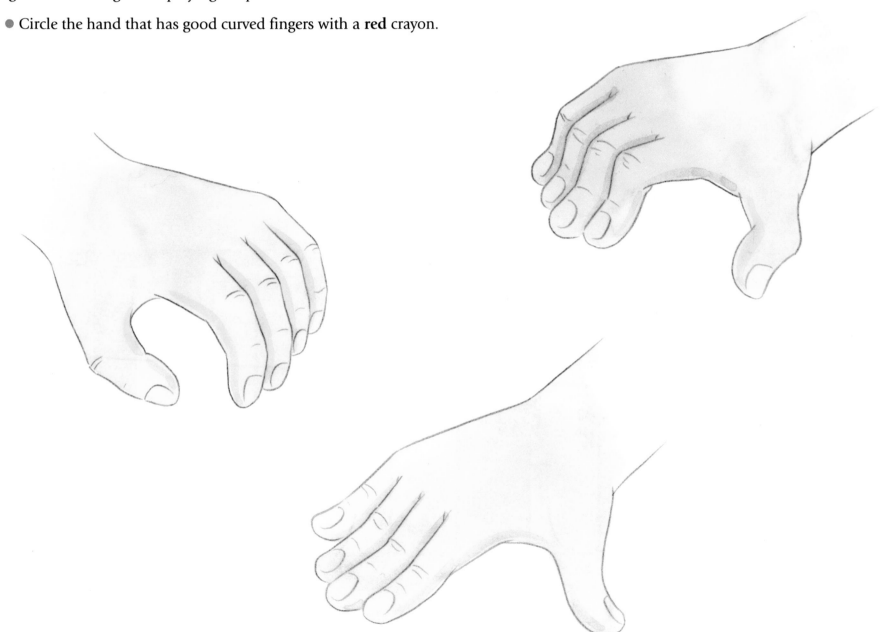

Low Sounds

Use with page 6.

Color the keys **blue** on the LEFT side of the keyboard
where Beethoven Bear likes to play LOW sounds.

High Sounds

Color the keys **red** on the RIGHT side of the keyboard
where Mozart Mouse likes to play HIGH sounds.

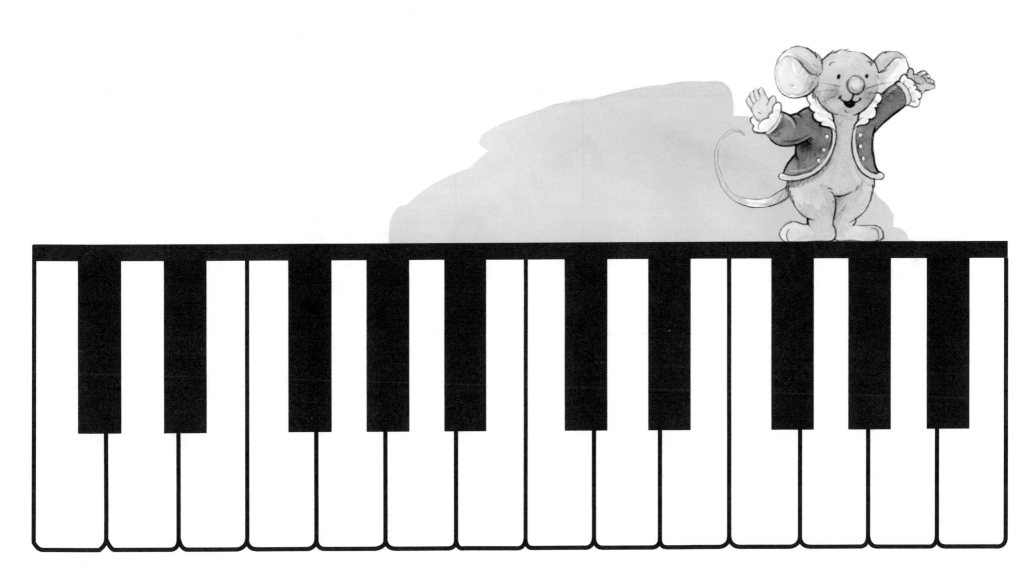

Use with page 7.

Low and High

Your teacher will play LOW and HIGH sounds.

- Circle Beethoven Bear if you hear a LOW sound.
- Circle Mozart Mouse if you hear a HIGH sound.

Up and Down

Your teacher will play sounds that go UP or DOWN.

● Circle Beethoven Bear walking UP the stairs if the sounds go UP.

● Circle Mozart Mouse walking DOWN the stairs if the sounds go DOWN.

Use with page 10.

Loud Sounds

Color the toys or animals from the playroom that make LOUD (f) sounds.
After your teacher checks your work, color the rest of the picture.

Soft Sounds

Color the toys or animals from the playroom that make soft (*p*) sounds. After your teacher checks your work, color the rest of the picture.

Use with page 12.

Left Hand Finger Numbers

Trace the numbers above each finger with a **black** crayon.

1 Color finger 1 (Thumbkin) **green**.

2 Color finger 2 (Pointer) **red**.

3 Color finger 3 (Tall Man) **blue**.

4 Color finger 4 (Ring Man) **purple**.

5 Color finger 5 (Pinky) **pink**.

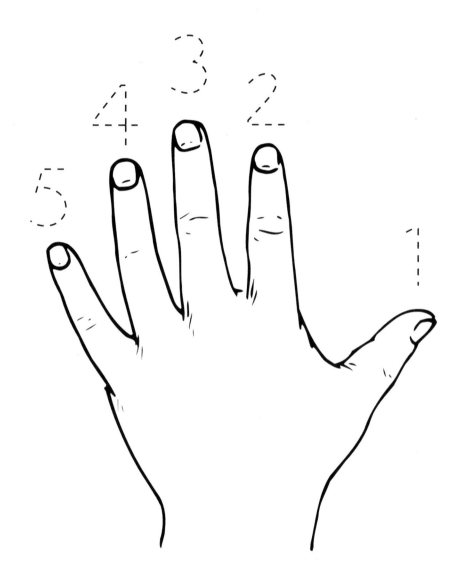

Right Hand Finger numbers

Trace the numbers above each finger with a **black** crayon.

1 Color finger 1 (Thumbkin) **green.**

2 Color finger 2 (Pointer) **red.**

3 Color finger 3 (Tall Man) **blue.**

4 Color finger 4 (Ring Man) **purple.**

5 Color finger 5 (Pinky) **pink.**

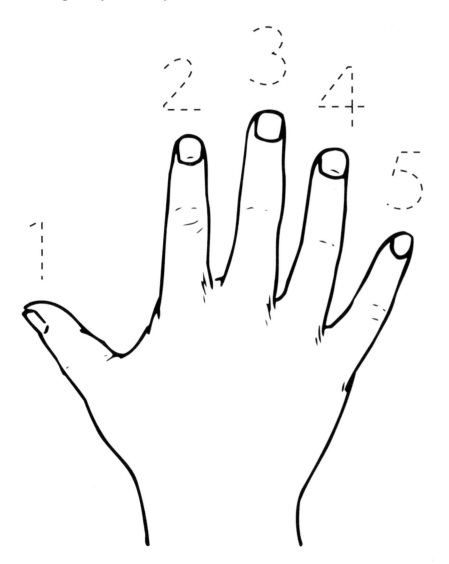

Use with page 14.

2 Black Keys

Help Beethoven Bear find all of the 2 BLACK KEY groups.

● Circle each group with a **red** crayon.

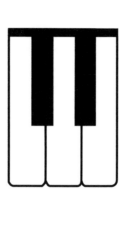

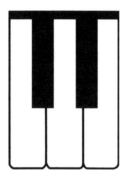

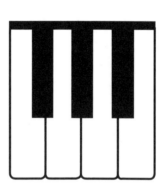

Quarter Note

1 Trace and color each QUARTER NOTE **black.**

2 A QUARTER NOTE gets 1 count. Color each 1 **red.**

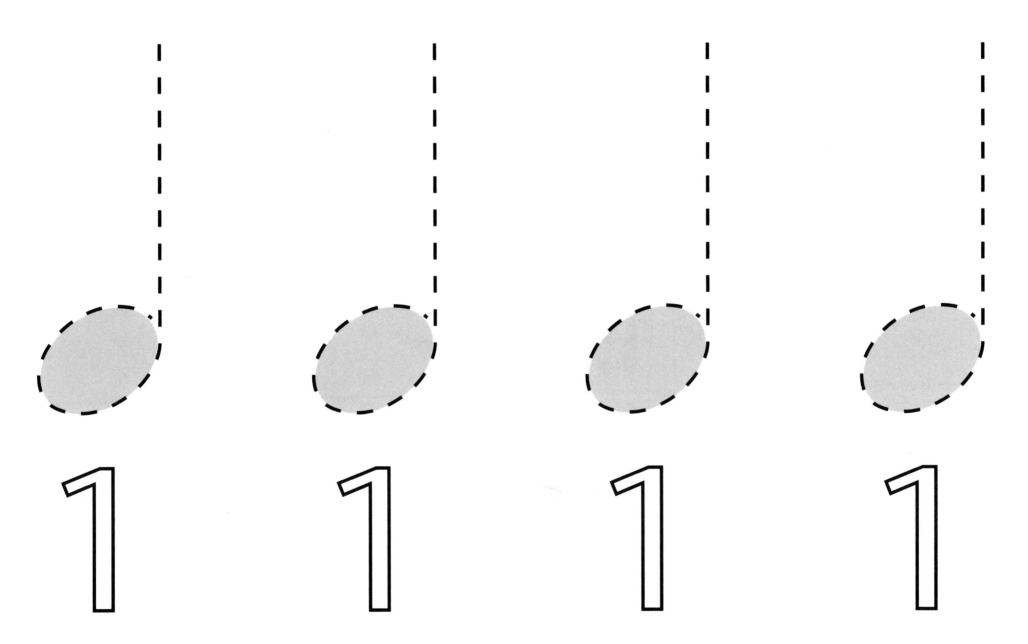

Quarter Notes and 2 Black Key Groups

Use with page 16.

1 Color the areas containing a QUARTER NOTE (♩) **red**.

2 Color the areas containing a 2 BLACK KEY GROUP **blue**.

Fingers 2 and 3

1. Color finger 2 **red** on each hand.

2. Color finger 3 **blue** on each hand.

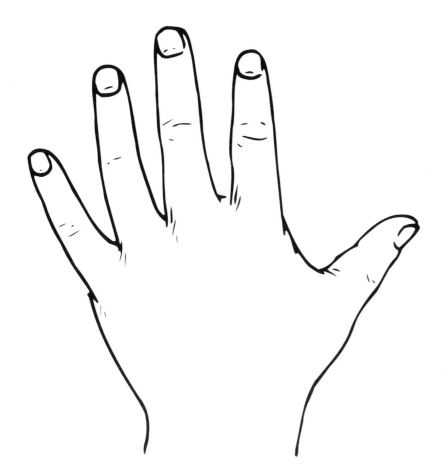

LEFT HAND

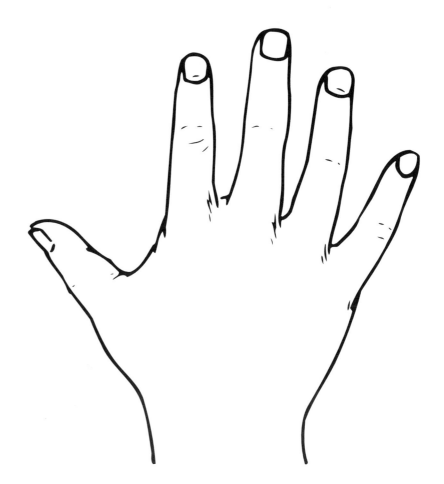

RIGHT HAND

Use with page 18.

3 Black Keys

Help Mozart Mouse find all of the 3 BLACK KEY groups.

● Circle each group with a **blue** crayon.

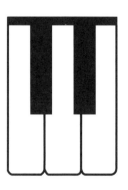

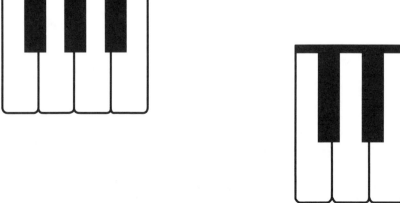

Quarter Rest

1 Trace and color each QUARTER REST **black.**

2 A QUARTER REST gets 1 count. Color each 1 **red.**

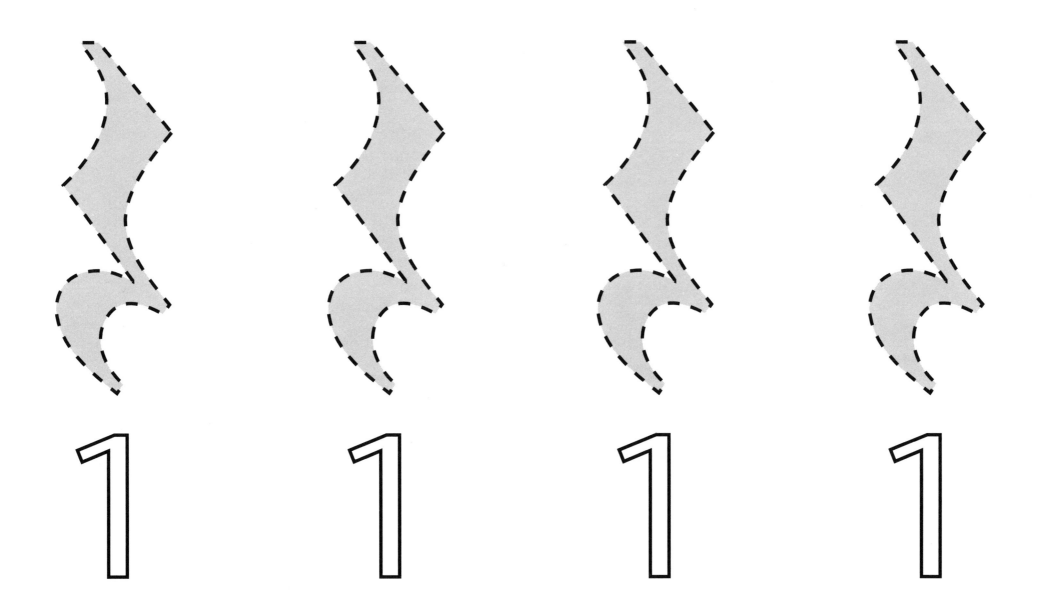

Use with page 20.

Quarter Rests and 3 Black Key Groups

1 Color the papers containing a QUARTER REST (𝄽) **pink**.

2 Color the papers containing a 3 BLACK KEY GROUP **yellow**.

Fingers 2, 3 and 4

1 Color finger 2 **red** on each hand.

2 Color finger 3 **blue** on each hand.

3 Color finger 4 **purple** on each hand.

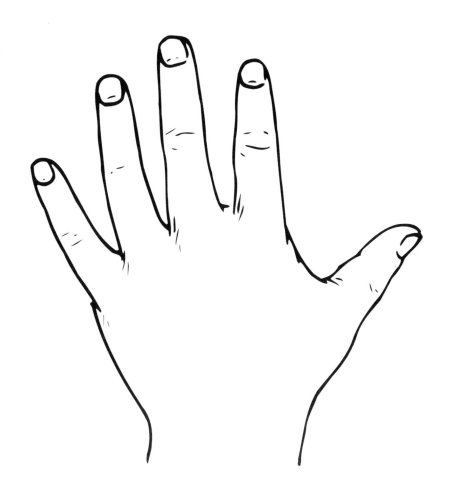

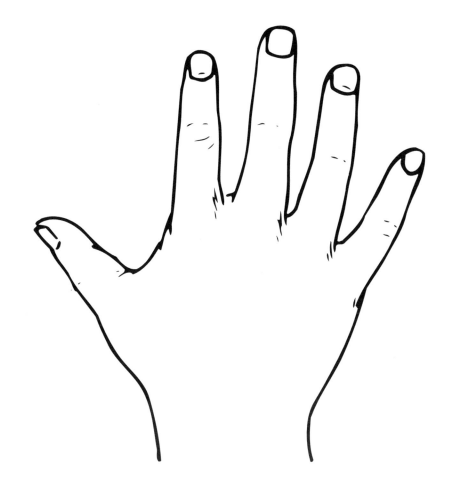

LEFT HAND

RIGHT HAND

Use with page 22.

Quarter Notes

Find and circle five QUARTER NOTES (♩) on *Old MacDonald's Farm.*

Quarter Rests

Find and circle five QUARTER RESTS (𝄽) on the *Pony Ride.*

Quarter Notes and Quarter Rests

Use with page 24.

Your teacher will clap a rhythm pattern.

● Circle the pattern that you hear.

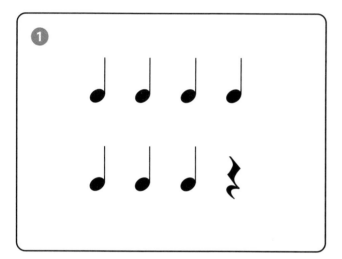

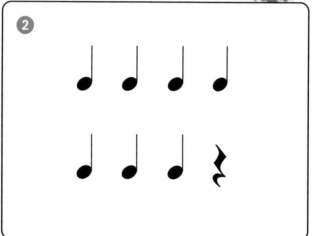

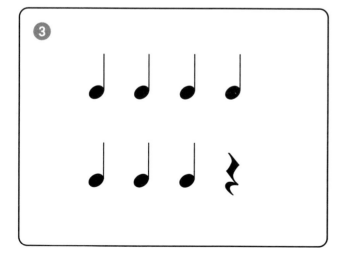

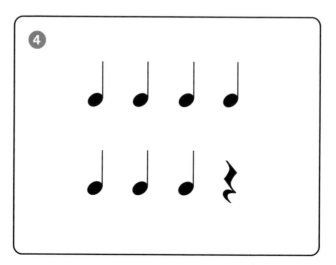

Up and Down

Your teacher will play patterns that go UP or DOWN.

- Circle the pattern that you hear.

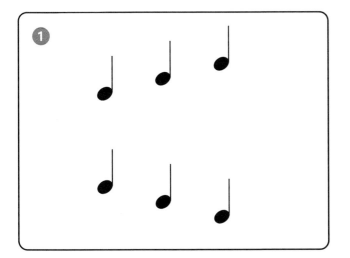

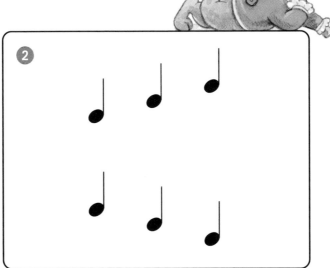

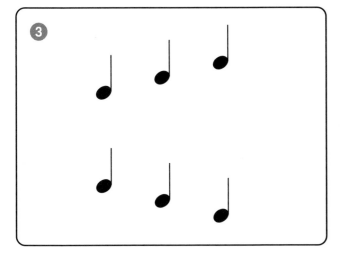

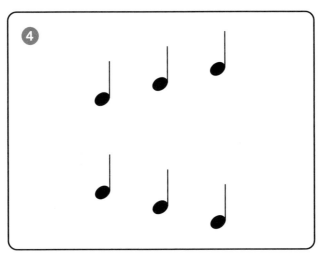

Finding D on the Keyboard

Use with page 26.

Help Beethoven Bear find each D on the keyboard.

- Draw a line from Beethoven Bear to each D.
- Color each D **yellow**.

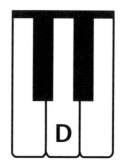

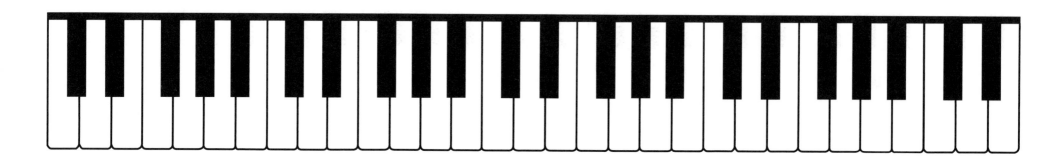

Finding High and Low D

1 Color the HIGHEST D **red.**

2 Color the LOWEST D **yellow.**

3 Color the other D's **blue.**

Use with page 28.

Finding C on the Keyboard

Help Mozart Mouse find each C on the keyboard.

- Draw a line from Mozart Mouse to each C.
- Color each C **green**.

Finding High and Low C

1 Color the HIGHEST C **green**.

2 Color the LOWEST C **purple**.

3 Color the other C's **brown**.

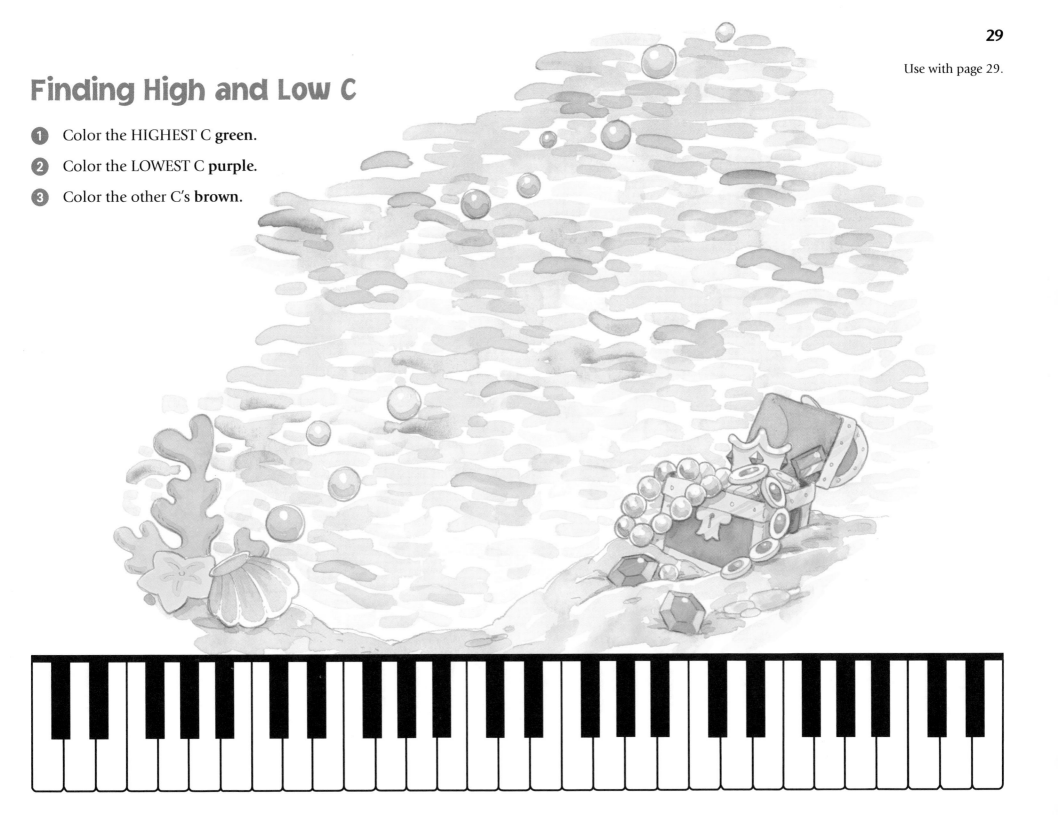

C and D

1 Color the areas containing a C **red.**

2 Color the areas containing a D **blue.**

Half Note

1 Trace each HALF NOTE with a **black** crayon.

2 A HALF NOTE gets 2 counts.
Color each 1 **red** and each 2 **blue.**

Use with page 32.

Finding E on the Keyboard

Help Mozart Mouse find each E on the keyboard.

- Draw a line from Mozart Mouse to each E.
- Color each E **red.**

E

Finding High and Low E

1. Color the HIGHEST E **pink.**

2. Color the LOWEST E **orange.**

3. Color the other E's **green.**

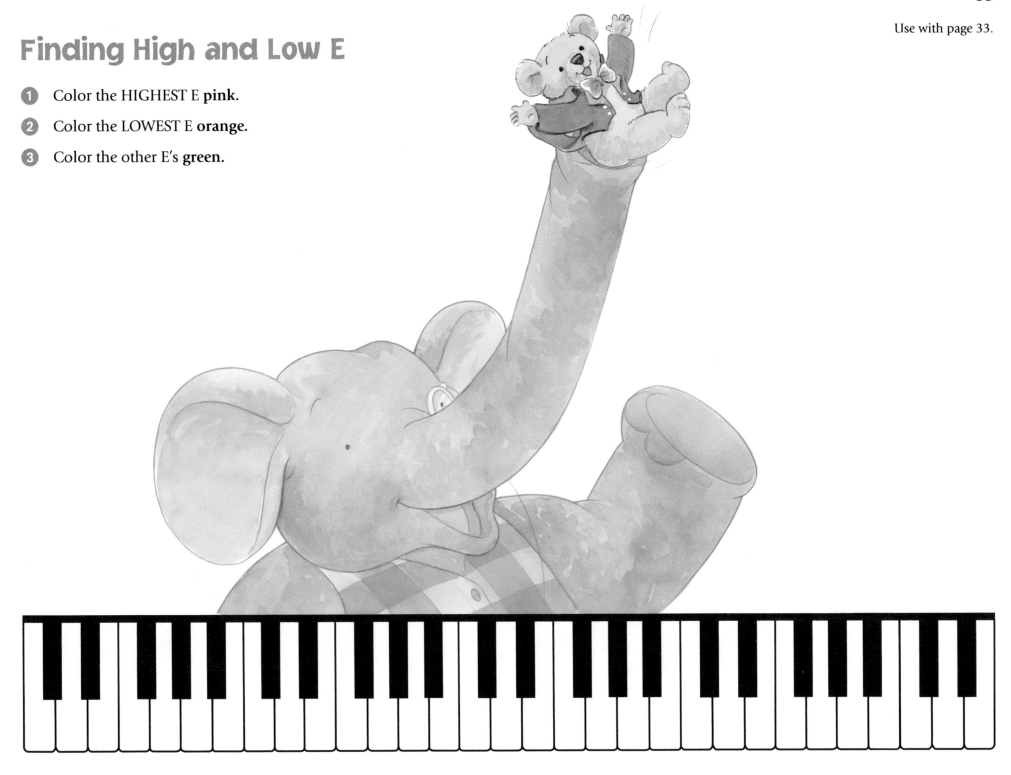

Use with page 34.

White Keys C, D, E

1. Color each C **yellow.**

2. Color each D **brown.**

3. Color each E **purple**

Half Rest

1 Trace and color each HALF REST **black**.

2 A HALF REST gets 2 counts.
Color each 1 **red** and each 2 **blue**.

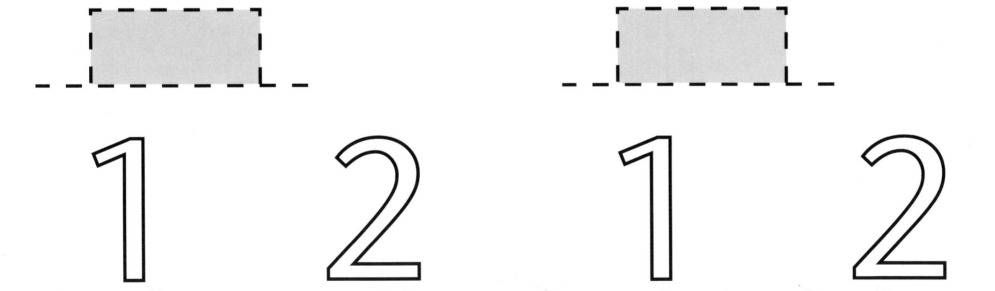

Half Notes and Half Rests

Your teacher will clap a rhythm pattern.

● Circle the pattern that you hear.

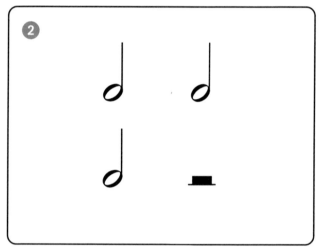

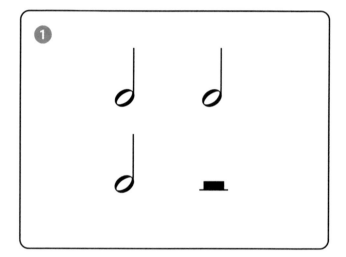

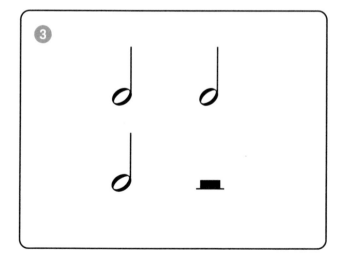

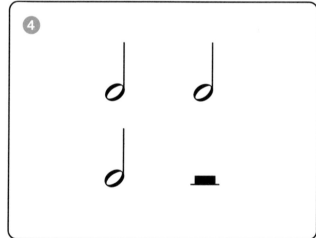

Playing C with Left Hand & Right Hand

1. Circle each C that is played by the LEFT HAND with a **pink** crayon.

2. Circle each C that is played by the RIGHT HAND with a **green** crayon.

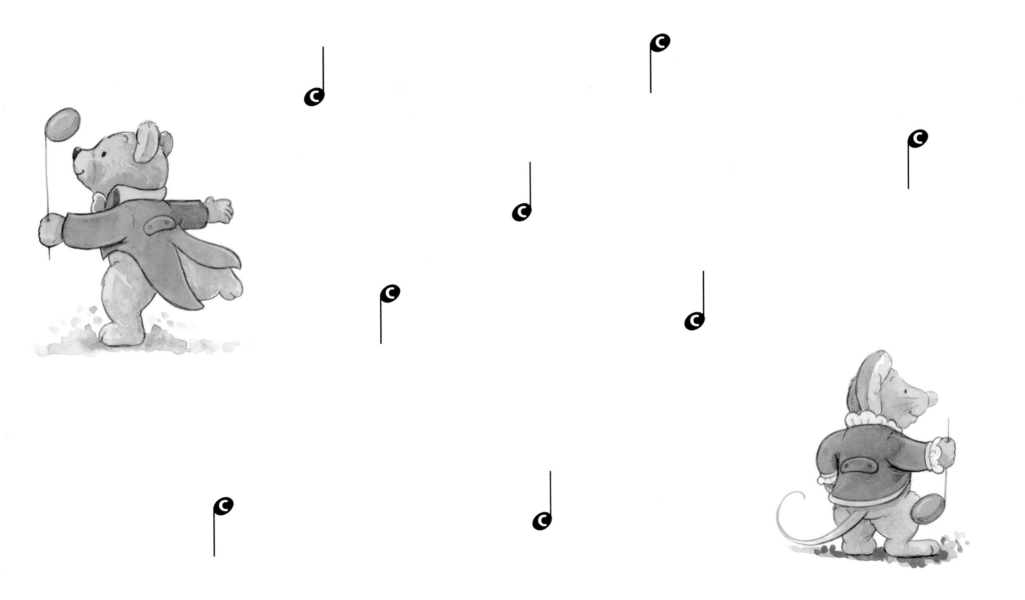

Use with page 38.

Finding B on the Keyboard

Help Beethoven Bear find each B on the keyboard.

- Draw a line from Beethoven Bear to each B.

- Color each B **purple**.

Finding High and Low B

1. Color the HIGHEST B **red.**

2. Color the LOWEST B **yellow.**

3. Color the other B's **blue.**

C and B

1. Color the areas containing a C **red**.
2. Color the areas containing a B **gray**.

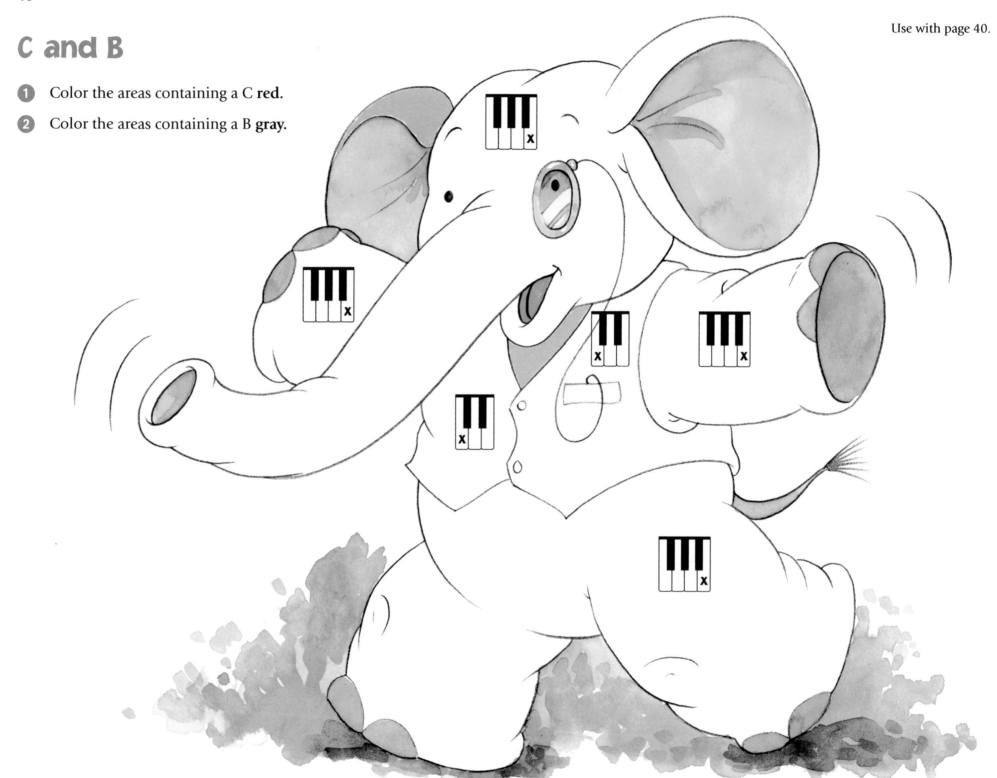

Whole Note

1 Trace the WHOLE NOTE with a **black** crayon.

2 A WHOLE NOTE gets 4 counts.
Color the 1 **red;** the 2 **blue;** the 3 **green** and the 4 **yellow.**

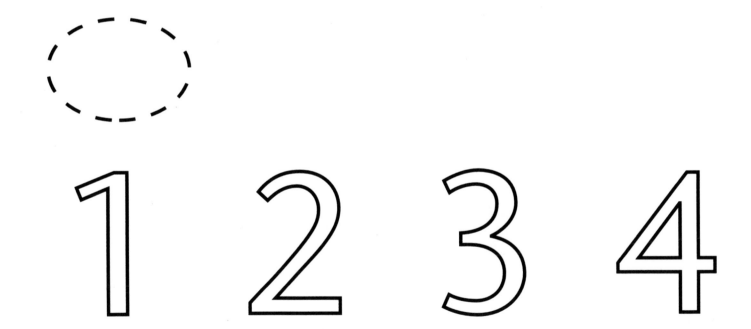

Finding A on the Keyboard

Use with page 42.

Help Beethoven Bear and Mozart Mouse find each A on the keyboard.

- Draw a line from Beethoven Bear or Mozart Mouse to each A.

- Color each A **blue**.

Finding High and Low A

1. Color the HIGHEST A **green**.

2. Color the LOWEST A **purple**.

3. Color the other A's **brown**.

Use with page 44.

White Keys A, B, C

1. Color each A **red**.

2. Color each B **blue**.

3. Color each C **yellow**.

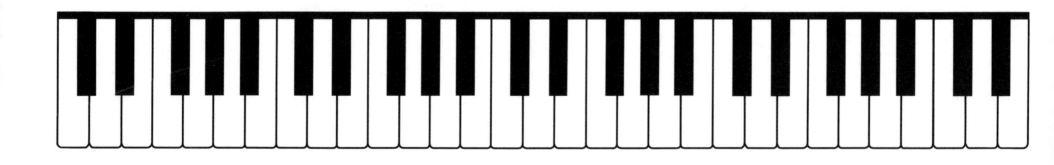

Whole Rest

1 Trace and color the WHOLE REST **black.**

2 A WHOLE REST gets 4 counts.
Color the 1 **red;** the 2 **blue;** the 3 **green** and the 4 **yellow.**

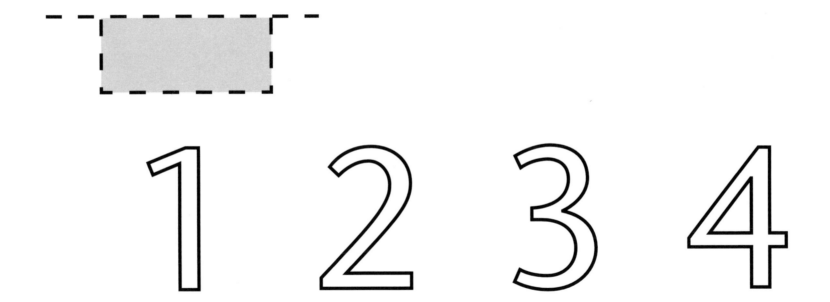

Use with page 46.

Middle C Position for the Left Hand

Color the C, B and A from the Left Hand MIDDLE C POSITION **blue.**

Middle C Position for the Right Hand

Color the C, D and E from the Right Hand MIDDLE C POSITION **red.**

Up and Down

Your teacher will play patterns that go UP or DOWN in the MIDDLE C POSITION.
- Circle the pattern that you hear.

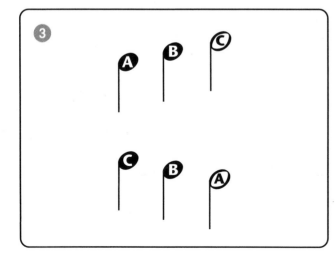

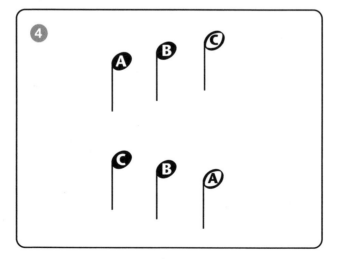

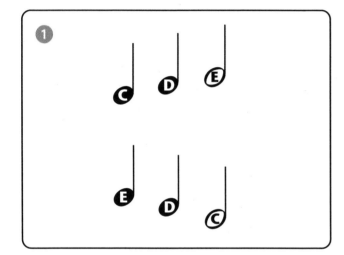

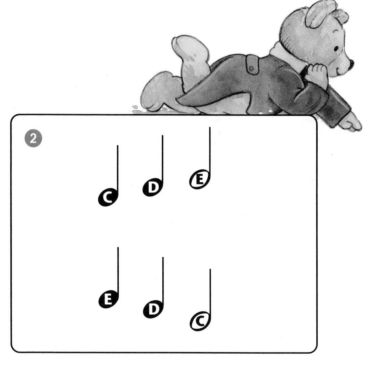